# Big Cats

# Leopard

Written by
Steve Goldsworthy

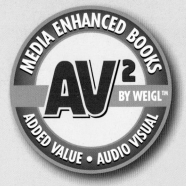

AV² provides enriched content that supplements and complements this book. Weigl's AV² books strive to create inspired learning and engage young minds in a total learning experience.

## Your AV² Media Enhanced books come alive with...

**Audio**
Listen to sections of the book read aloud.

**Key Words**
Study vocabulary, and complete a matching word activity.

**Video**
Watch informative video clips.

**Quizzes**
Test your knowledge.

Go to **www.av2books.com**, and enter this book's unique code.

## BOOK CODE

U 1 3 2 2 2 6

**Embedded Weblinks**
Gain additional information for research.

**Slide Show**
View images and captions, and prepare a presentation.

**AV² by Weigl** brings you media enhanced books that support active learning.

**Try This!**
Complete activities and hands-on experiments.

**... and much, much more!**

Published by AV² by Weigl
350 5th Avenue, 59th Floor
New York, NY 10118
Websites: www.av2books.com    www.weigl.com

Library of Congress Cataloging-in-Publication Data

Goldsworthy, Steve, author.
 Leopard / Steve Goldsworthy.
    pages cm. -- (Big cats)
 Includes index.
 ISBN 978-1-4896-0922-9 (hardcover : alk. paper) -- ISBN 978-1-4896-0923-6 (softcover : alk. paper) -- ISBN 978-1-4896-0924-3 (single user ebk.) -- ISBN 978-1-4896-0925-0 (multi user ebk.)
 1. Leopard--Juvenile literature. I. Title.
 QL737.C23G644 2015
 599.75'54--dc23

2014004319

Printed in the United States of America in North Mankato, Minnesota
1 2 3 4 5 6 7 8 9 0  18 17 16 15 14

032014
WEP150314

Editor Heather Kissock     Design Terry Paulhus

Photo Credits
Weigl acknowledges Getty Images as its primary photo supplier for this title.

# Contents

# Meet the Leopard

Leopards are **mammals** that belong to the **Panthera** cat group. This group includes such big cats as tigers, lions, and jaguars. The leopard is the strongest climber in the big cat family. Leopards spend most of their time in trees, which is where they sleep and eat. Leopards eat a wide variety of animals, from birds and snakes to large deer species. Sometimes, they even eat chimpanzees and baboons.

Leopards are most active at night. This is also when they do most of their hunting. They sleep during the day. Spots on a leopard's coat make the cat very hard to see. It can hide among a tree's leaves or wait for **prey** in tall grasses.

*Panthera pardus* is the scientific name for the leopard.

# All About
# Leopards

The leopard is a member of the *felidae* group of animals. This family includes all cats ranging from tigers to house cats. There are nine **subspecies** of leopard. These include the African leopard, the Indian leopard, the Arabian leopard, and the North Chinese leopard. Scientists once considered black panthers a separate species. After closer examination, scientists determined that the black panther is actually a black leopard. It has black spots that are only visible up close.

Leopards make their homes in many regions throughout the world. They can be found in parts of Central Asia, India, and China. The largest leopard population is in Africa. Leopards live in more than 35 African countries, including Mozambique, Namibia, Tanzania, and Uganda.

Similar to human fingerprints, a leopard's spot patterns are individually unique.

# Comparing Big Cats

The leopard is one of the smallest animals in the big cat family. All big cats have unique traits that help them survive. The lion uses its size and strength to hunt, while the cheetah relies on its speed. The leopard uses **stealth** to hide in its surroundings and sneak up on its prey.

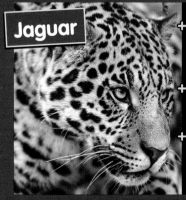

**Jaguar**

+ **Length:**
7–9 feet
(213–274 centimeters)
including tail
+ **Weight:**
100–250 pounds
(45–113 kilograms)
+ **Speed:**
Up to 40 miles per hour
(64 kilometers
per hour)

**Lion**

+ **Length:**
6.5–9 feet
(198–274 cm)
including tail
+ **Weight:**
265–420 lbs
(120–190 kg)
+ **Speed:**
Up to 35 mph (56 kph)

**Tiger**

+ **Length:**
7.5–10.8 feet
(260–330 cm)
including tail
+ **Weight:**
220–675 pounds
(100–306 kg)
+ **Speed:**
Up to 40 mph (64 kph)

**Leopard**

+ **Length:**
6.5–9 feet
(198–274 cm)
including tail
+ **Weight:**
66–176 lbs (30–80 kg)
+ **Speed:**
Up to 57 mph (92 kph)

**Cheetah**

+ **Length:**
6–7 feet
(183– 213 cm)
including tail
+ **Weight:**
77–143 lbs  (35–65 kg)
+ **Speed:**
Up to 70 mph
(112 kph)

**Cougar**

+ **Length:**
5–9 feet
(152–274 cm)
including tail
+ **Weight:**
Up to 150 lbs (68 kg)
+ **Speed:**
Up to 35 mph (56 kph)

# Leopard
# History

Leopards share a common **ancestor** with lions, tigers, jaguars, and snow leopards. This ancestor lived more than 6 million years ago in Asia. Scientists have discovered **fossil** evidence that leopards existed in Tanzania 3.5 million years ago.

Evidence of leopards can also be found in several ancient cultures. Ancient Greeks and Egyptians wore leopard skins during religious rituals. Ancient Egyptians considered the leopard sacred because it represented the sky-goddess Mafdet. Ancient Romans brought leopards from Africa to use as entertainment in their arenas.

Leopards once roamed dozens of countries, from England all the way to Japan. The leopard is now **extinct** in many countries and is at risk in several others. However, its population is rising thanks to **conservation** efforts.

England
Japan
Egypt
PACIFIC OCEAN
INDIAN OCEAN

## FIRST BIG CAT

Today's big cats **evolved** from an animal called *pseudaelurus* that roamed Earth about 20 million years ago.

The rarest species of big cat is the Amur leopard. Experts say there are fewer than 50 living in the wild.

# Where Leopards Live

The leopard adapts easily, which is key to its survival. It can live in a range of climates and **habitats**, such as rainforests and deserts. Leopards like to live in areas with plenty of bushes and trees, but they also do well in rocky areas. These habitats provide the leopard with high places that make hunting easier. The leopards can jump on their prey from branches and high rocks.

The leopard is an excellent climber and uses trees to its advantage. Branches cover it when it is hunting. It also uses trees to hide and eat its kill. Male leopards have a large territory that can cover up to 25 square miles (40 square kilometers). They will often mark their territory with urine and with claw marks on trees.

# SWIMMING CATS

Leopards often live near rivers, where they will swim to find food. Fish and crabs are just two animals that they catch.

A female leopard's territory is much smaller than that of a male.

# Leopard Features

The leopard is a very strong animal, especially for its small size. It has short, muscular legs, and its body is longer than most big cats. The leopard has a broad head and a powerful jaw. A leopard's spotted coat serves as **camouflage**. The spots help leopards hide among leaves and tall grasses.

②

④

# Getting Closer

## ① Eyes

- Superior eyesight
- Strong night vision

## ② Coat

- Light gold and white
- Covered with black-and-gold spots called **rosettes**
- Shape of spots varies by region

## ③ Throat

- Can roar due to structure of throat
- Also purrs, growls, and barks to communicate

## ④ Hind Legs

- Very powerful legs
- Used to leap into high trees
- Allow leopards to carry heavy prey up trees

## ⑤ Paws

- Sharp claws aid climbing
- Have **retractable** claws

# What Do Leopards Eat?

**L**eopards are **carnivores**, and they are not picky about the meat they eat. A leopard will kill and eat almost any animal it can find. Leopards' main prey includes antelope, wild pigs, and deer. If they can catch them, leopards also eat impalas, wildebeest, hares, and goats. Leopards sometimes eat animals that other predators kill.

The leopard is a mostly **nocturnal** hunter. It uses its sharp eyesight to find animals at night, catching prey by surprise. The leopard has extra-long whiskers. These help a leopard feel its way through tall grasses at night.

A leopard can carry an animal three times its own body weight up a tree. This protects the kill from other **predators**. The leopard often leaves its prey in a tree for days and will return to eat the animal over time.

## FOOD FIGHT

Lions, cheetahs, and hyenas are a few of the predators that compete with the leopard for food.

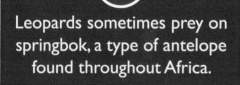

Leopards sometimes prey on springbok, a type of antelope found throughout Africa.

# Leopard
# Life Cycle

**A**dult leopards are **solitary** animals and roam in their own territories. Males and females come together when it is time to mate. Females signal that they are ready to mate by leaving their scent on trees.

## Birth to 2 Weeks

Baby leopards, known as cubs, are gray and do not have spots at birth. They are born with their eyes closed. The cubs open their eyes after four to nine days. A mother leopard must constantly move her litter to protect the cubs from predators.

Male leopards are old enough to mate by age 3, but they must often compete with other males. A female leopard is ready to mate by age 2. The **gestation** period for a pregnant leopard is 2.5 months. She will typically give birth to one to three cubs, called a litter.

## 2 Years and Older

Male leopards begin to hunt for themselves by age 2. They are fully grown by the age of 3. This is when they establish a hunting territory and look for a mate. Females live with their mother longer.

A leopard can live up to 14 years in the nature, but it may survive longer in captivity. Some leopards have lived up to 21 years in zoos and other facilities.

## 2 Weeks to 2 Years

Leopard cubs learn hunting techniques from their mother. They play-fight with each other, which is how they practice their hunting skills. Cubs first eat meat at about 6 weeks old. They drink milk until their mother **weans** them at about 3 months. The cubs live with their mother until age 2 to ensure they have mastered hunting and survival techniques.

# Leopard
# Conservation

There are more leopards in the wild than tigers or lions. Some scientists believe there are as many as 250,000 leopards throughout the world. Most live in Africa. Conservationists are concerned this number is dropping because of increased hunting.

Humans hunt leopards for their spotted fur. Most hunters sell the fur to make coats or ceremonial robes. Others kill leopards when **trophy hunting**. Many ranchers kill leopards to keep their animals safe from the big cats.

Some countries have established rules for hunting leopards. Other countries have outlawed all leopard hunting to help save the leopard population.

Organizations such as the African Wildlife Foundation help protect leopards. They study the African population of leopards by counting them and tracking where they live.

## LOW NUMBERS

The International Union for Conservation of Nature considers leopards a near-threatened species.

Deforestation and a loss of food sources also contribute to the decreasing leopard population.

# Myths and Legends

The leopard has been included in myths and legends for centuries. In Greek mythology, the god Dionysus rode a leopard and wore leopard skin as a cape. Leopards traveled everywhere with Dionysus, as the god taught people valuable lessons. Many Europeans believe that the leopard signifies fierceness. This is why noble families in Germany have used images of leopards in their **coats of arms**.

A story from the African country of Sierra Leone explains why leopards have spots. According to this story, Leopard's wife suggested he invite their friend, Fire, to visit. Fire was very excited to come and danced around Leopard's house with joy. Before long, Leopard's house was on fire. Leopard tried desperately to save his house, scorching his beige coat. His spots are a lesson to others not to play with fire.

Many cultures have stories about how the leopard came to have spots. These stories are passed down from generation to generation.

# Leopard Population Map

Scientists study the population of leopards throughout the world. This information helps them understand leopard behavior and movement. It also helps conservationists monitor the leopard's survival and learn which habitats best suit it. Scientists learn how humans might be threatening a leopard's habitat. You can make your own leopard population map to learn more about this big cat.

**Materials needed:** You will need a blank map of the world, a piece of paper big enough to fit the map, some glue, and markers in four colors.

 **STEP 1** Make a copy of a blank map of the world. Find one on the internet or copy one from a book. Glue it to the large piece of paper.

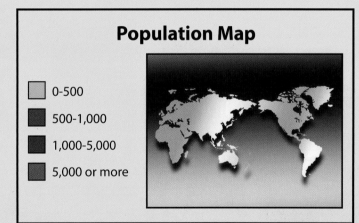

**Population Map**

- ☐ 0-500
- ■ 500-1,000
- ■ 1,000-5,000
- ■ 5,000 or more

 **STEP 2** Draw, color, and label four boxes as follows: blue 0–500, purple 500–1,000, red 1,000–5,000, pink 5,000 or more.

 **STEP 3** Start with the information in this book, and then use the internet to research the world population of leopards. Identify the countries where leopards are found. Using the population "key" you made in Step 2, color each country in the world with the color matching the number of leopards found there. Can you see where leopards might be endangered? Are there more leopards in hotter countries?

# 5 Know Your FACTS

## Test your knowledge of leopards.

**1** To which cat group does the leopard belong?

**2** Which continent has the highest population of leopards?

**3** Which species of big cat is the rarest?

**4** What are a leopard's spots called?

**5** Which Greek god rode on the backs of leopards?

**ANSWERS**

**1** Panthera
**2** Africa
**3** The Amur leopard
**4** Rosettes
**5** Dionysus

# Key Words

**ancestor:** a relative that lived long ago

**camouflage:** markings on an animal's coat that help it blend into its surroundings

**carnivores:** animals that eat other animals

**coats of arms:** designs on and around shields or on drawings of shields

**conservation:** the protection of animals

**evolved:** changed over time

**extinct:** no longer existing

**fossil:** prehistoric remains, such as bones and teeth

**gestation:** the length of time a female animal is pregnant

**habitats:** the natural areas where animals live

**mammals:** animals that are warm-blooded, born alive, and drink milk from their mother

**nocturnal:** active at night

**Panthera:** a class of animal that includes leopards, lions, tigers, jaguars, and snow leopards

**predators:** animals they naturally prey on other animals

**prey:** an animal that is killed by another animal for food

**retractable:** able to draw back

**rosettes:** rose-shaped markings or spots

**solitary:** animals that live alone, not in groups

**stealth:** to move slowly and quietly; to be undetected

**subspecies:** a subdivision of species, typically a geographical or ecological subdivision

**trophy hunting:** the hunting of wild game animals

**weans:** to slowly stop feeding a young animal milk from its mother

# Index

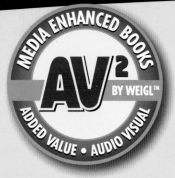

# Log on to www.av2books.com

AV² by Weigl brings you media enhanced books that support active learning. Go to www.av2books.com, and enter the special code found on page 2 of this book. You will gain access to enriched and enhanced content that supplements and complements this book. Content includes video, audio, weblinks, quizzes, a slide show, and activities.

## AV² Online Navigation

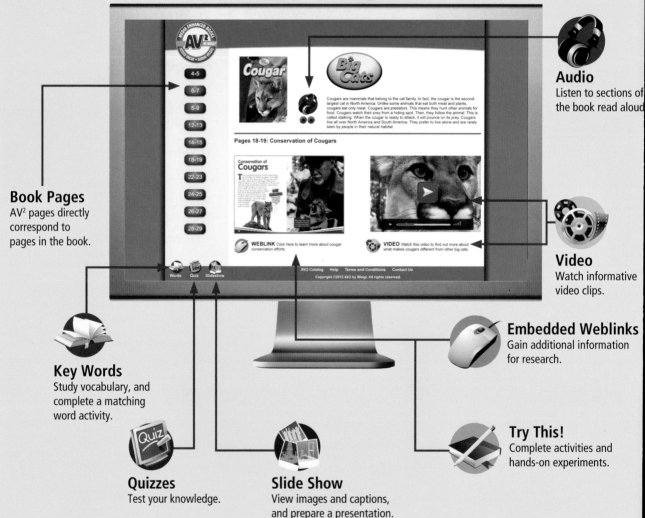

**Audio**
Listen to sections of the book read aloud

**Book Pages**
AV² pages directly correspond to pages in the book.

**Video**
Watch informative video clips.

**Embedded Weblinks**
Gain additional information for research.

**Key Words**
Study vocabulary, and complete a matching word activity.

**Try This!**
Complete activities and hands-on experiments.

**Quizzes**
Test your knowledge.

**Slide Show**
View images and captions, and prepare a presentation.

---

AV² was built to bridge the gap between print and digital. We encourage you to tell us what you like and what you want to see in the future.

## Sign up to be an AV² Ambassador at www.av2books.com/ambassador.

Due to the dynamic nature of the Internet, some of the URLs and activities provided as part of AV² by Weigl may have changed or ceased to exist. AV² by Weigl accepts no responsibility for any such changes. All media enhanced books are regularly monitored to update addresses and sites in a timely manner. Contact AV² by Weigl at 1-866-649-3445 or av2books@weigl.com with any questions, comments, or feedback.